8 contemporary pieces
for CELLO and PIANO

GW00645216

UNBEATEN TRACKS

Edited by Steven Isserlis

CONTENTS

© 2000 by Faber Music Ltd
First published in 2000 by Faber Music Ltd
3 Queen Square London WC1N 3AU
Cover design by Økvik Design
Music processed by Wessex Music Services
Printed in England by Caligraving Ltd
All rights reserved

ISBN 0-571-51976-8

To buy Faber Music publications or to find out about the
full range of titles available please contact your local music
retailer or Faber Music sales enquiries:
Faber Music Ltd, Burnt Mill, Elizabeth Way, Harlow CM20 2HX
Tel: +44 (0)1279 82 89 82   Fax: +44 (0)1279 82 89 83
sales@fabermusic.com   www.fabermusic.com

Elegy

Carl Davis

for Steven Isserlis

Album leaf, Op. 66

Lowell Liebermann

Andante piacevole, con molto rubato (♩ = *c*.88)

to Gabriel Isserlis

Frogs dancing on water lilies

Olli Mustonen

Cantilena

John Woolrich

for Steven Isserlis

Hip hip bourrée

Julian Jacobson

Vocalise

Mark-Anthony Turnage

Tango flageoletto

David Matthews

to Gabriel – of course!

The Haunted House

Steven Isserlis

12

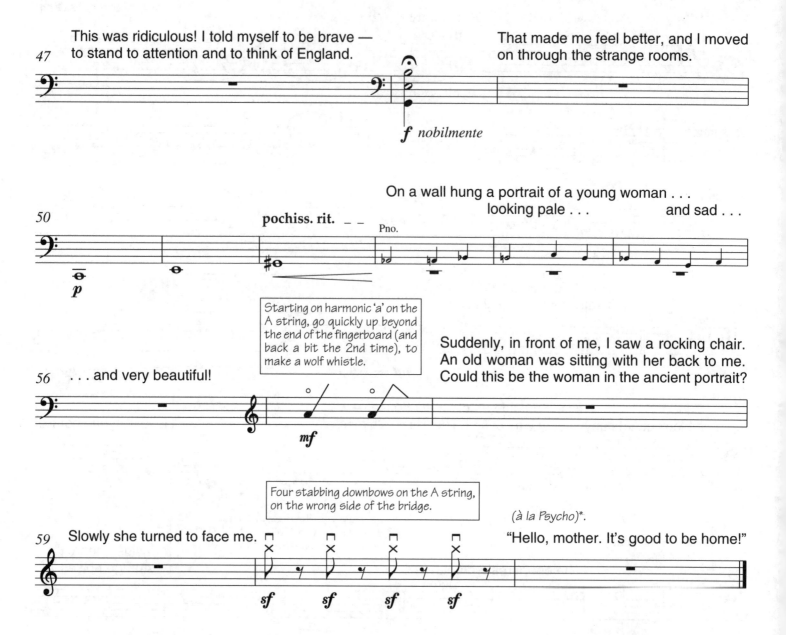

This was ridiculous! I told myself to be brave —
to stand to attention and to think of England.

That made me feel better, and I moved
on through the strange rooms.

f nobilmente

On a wall hung a portrait of a young woman . . .
looking pale . . .   and sad . . .

pochiss. rit. _ _

Pno.

p

Starting on harmonic 'a' on the
A string, go quickly up beyond
the end of the fingerboard (and
back a bit the 2nd time), to
make a wolf whistle.

Suddenly, in front of me, I saw a rocking chair.
An old woman was sitting with her back to me.
Could this be the woman in the ancient portrait?

. . . and very beautiful!

mf

Four stabbing downbows on the A string,
on the wrong side of the bridge.

(à la Psycho)*.

Slowly she turned to face me.

"Hello, mother. It's good to be home!"

sf   *sf*   *sf*   *sf*

* A wonderfully creepy film directed by Alfred Hitchcock.

8 contemporary pieces

for CELLO and PIANO

UNBEATEN TRACKS

Edited by Steven Isserlis

© 2000 by Faber Music Ltd
First published in 2000 by Faber Music Ltd
3 Queen Square London WC1N 3AU
Cover design by Økvik Design
Music processed by Wessex Music Services
Printed in England by Caligraving Ltd
All rights reserved

ISBN 0-571-51976-8

To buy Faber Music publications or to find out about the
full range of titles available please contact your local music
retailer or Faber Music sales enquiries:
Faber Music Ltd, Burnt Mill, Elizabeth Way, Harlow CM20 2HX
Tel: +44 (0)1279 82 89 82   Fax: +44 (0)1279 82 89 83
sales@fabermusic.com   www.fabermusic.com

FABER *ff* MUSIC

PREFACE

I am delighted with this collection of weird and wonderful pieces – a collection that I hope will come to be viewed as staple repertoire for cello students, as well as fascinating encores for professionals (I'm already performing several of them regularly). One of the qualities that I find most appealing in this volume is the variety of musical personalities that shine through each offering: Mark-Anthony Turnage, Lowell Liebermann and John Woolrich are all seen at their most poetic and melancholic; Olli Mustonen characteristically alternates between reflection and exuberance; David Matthews enjoys an exotic knees-up; Carl Davis enjoys a romantic melt; and Julian Jacobson and I provide the comic relief with (respectively) a merry Bach-pastiche and a thoroughly unsubtle tribute to that other master of the Baroque, Alfred Hitchcock.

The fingerings and bowings are just suggestions; if they don't suit you, use your own!

Steven Isserlis

COMPOSER BIOPICS

All contributing composers were asked to give their own personal response to the following; of course their answers can only reflect their views now and will be ever-changing:

Date and Place of Birth

Musical works that have most inspired you

Individuals who have most inspired you

What your piece means to you

A quote that you feel best describes your music in general

Your two favourite books

Carl Davis

Date and Place of Birth	28.10.36 New York
Inspiring musical works	*B minor Mass*, Johann Sebastian Bach *West Side Story*, Leonard Bernstein
Inspiring individuals	Leonard Bernstein, Dietrich Fischer-Dieskau
What your piece means to you	The cello is one of the most expressive and warm instruments in all music. Played with proper feeling and understanding it can move you to tears. The 'Elegy' tries to use the cello for its ability to play long lines and to simply pour out sound. Imagine the piano is a guitar and that you're on holiday in the Mediterranean …
A quote	'… his music has a power that has you clutching the arms of your seat lest you be blown away' (*The Observer*)
Two favourite books	*Middlemarch*, George Eliot *The Catcher in the Rye*, J. D. Salinger

Lowell Liebermann

Date and Place of Birth	22.2.61 New York City
Inspiring musical works	*Symphony No.15*, *String quartet No.13*, Dmitry Shostakovich; *Doktor Faust*, Ferruccio Busoni; *'Jedermann' Lieder*, Frank Martin; *Piano Quintet* or *String Quintet*, *Drei Klavierstücke*, Franz Schubert; *Death in Venice*, Benjamin Britten
Inspiring individuals	Ada Sohn Segal (my childhood piano teacher); Friedelind Wagner; Stephen Hough; Sir Thomas More; James Galway; William Hobbs; and of course Steven Isserlis
What your piece means to you	The piece is based on a short sketch, a small fragment of a couple of measures that has haunted me for years without ever finding its completion. When Steven asked me for a short cello piece I looked again at the sketch, and suddenly knew that it would be the new cello piece. Uncompleted sketches are a bit like ghosts that are looking for their final rest, and I was very happy to finally complete this one.
A quote	'I have an almost moralistic view of the purpose of music and art in general: I think the cliché that art should reflect its time is sheer nonsense. Art should point to a more perfect world and lead humanity there.'
Two favourite books	*Extraordinary Popular Delusions and the Madness of Crowds*, Charles Mackay *The Picture of Dorian Gray*, Oscar Wilde

Olli Mustonen

Date and Place of Birth	7.6.67 Helsinki
Inspiring musical works	*Das wohltemperirte Klavier*, Johann Sebastian Bach; *Violin Concerto No.2*, Béla Bartók; *Grosse Fuge (String Quartet)*, Ludwig van Beethoven; *Piano Concerto No.1 in D minor*, Johannes Brahms; *Tapiola*, Jean Sibelius; *24 Preludes and Fugues*, Dmitry Shostakovich; *Cello Concerto*, Rodion Shchedrin
Inspiring individuals	Sándor Végh, Nikolaus Harnoncourt, Rodion Shchedrin, Steven Isserlis, my parents, my teachers, my wife
What your piece means to you	I guess if a composer decides to call his work 'Frogs dancing on water lilies' and not 'After Reading Wittgenstein' for instance, it might give the listener a subtle hint on the philosophical background of that composition! I suppose one could see it as a musical description of some mysteriously beautiful water lilies, which are suddenly interrupted by some musical but rather silly frogs.
Two favourite books	*Seven Brothers*, Aleksis Kivi *Hyperspace*, Michio Kaku

John Woolrich

Date and Place of Birth	3.1.54 Cirencester
Inspiring musical works	*Sestina*, Claudio Monteverdi *3 Pieces for String Quartet*, Igor Stravinsky *Marriage of Figaro*, Wolfgang Amadeus Mozart *Dichterliebe*, Robert Schumann
What your piece means to you	The cello is the instrument most like the human voice and prospers when it is allowed to 'sing'. This song for cello exploits the lyrical tenor register and the shadowy bass.
A quote	'His music whispers, whirrs, rustles, creaks, and shines with a gentle light, often elegiacal … Its characteristic movement is shy, blinking in the sun, attuned better to half lights' (Robin Holloway)
Two favourite books	*The Golden Pot*, E. T. A. Hoffmann *Tristram Shandy*, Laurence Sterne

Julian Jacobson

Date and Place of Birth	18.11.47 Peebles
Inspiring musical works	*La valse*, Maurice Ravel; *Sinfonia concertante*, Wolfgang Amadeus Mozart; *Where the wild things are*, Oliver Knussen; *Embraceable you*, George Gershwin (as played by Charlie Parker)
Inspiring individuals	Martha Argerich, McCoy Tyner, Wilfrid Mellers
What your piece means to you	I love writing in dance rhythms (waltzes, tangos, etc.). As friends know, I am also a devotee of atrocious puns – the title of this piece came to me unbidden and the music followed suit. Dedicated to many young cellists in general and one slightly older cellist in particular – Steven Isserlis.
A quote	'It sounds better than it looks'
Two favourite books	*Captain Corelli's Mandolin*, Louis de Bernières *The Pianoplayers*, Anthony Burgess

David Matthews

Date and Place of Birth	9.3.43 London
Inspiring musical works	*String Quartet in C sharp minor, Op.131*, Ludwig van Beethoven; *Tapiola*, Jean Sibelius; *Jack the Bear*, Duke Ellington
Inspiring individuals	Michael Tippett
What your piece means to you	Some years ago I wrote a tango as one of the movements of my Fourth Symphony, imagining it as a kind of contemporary equivalent to the classical minuet. I am fond of this piece, and it therefore became the inspiration for my Tango for cello. Of all contemporary dances, the tango seems to me the most exotic and alluring.
A quote	'Full of dark poetry and haunted vistas'
Two favourite books	Many favourites, but among them are *Fictions*, Jorge Luis Borges; *Ulysses*, James Joyce

Mark-Anthony Turnage

Date and Place of Birth	10.6.60 Corringham, Essex
Inspiring musical works	*Miles Ahead*, Miles Davis; *Billy Budd*, Benjamin Britten; *Symphony of Psalms*, Igor Stravinsky; *Case of You*, Joni Mitchell
Inspiring individuals	Oliver Knussen, John Scofield, Peter Erskine, Simon Rattle, Miles Davis, Joni Mitchell
What your piece means to you	A little melancholic ditty
A quote	'Mark-Anthony Turnage has rapidly earned a unique position among composers of his generation for his distinctly lyrical compositional voice, his ability to create complex yet lucid instrumental textures, and his innate dramatic sense'
Two favourite books	*The Brutality of Fact (interviews with Francis Bacon)*, David Sylvester; *The End of the Affair*, Graham Greene

Steven Isserlis

Date and Place of Birth	19.12.58 London
Inspiring musical works	Too numerous to mention!
Inspiring individuals	The Beatles, The Marx Brothers, Robert Schumann, the Monty Python Team, Pablo Casals, Members of Spïnal Tap, Daniil Shafran, Wilkie Collins, various friends, relatives and colleagues whose heads would get too big if I mentioned them
What your piece means to you	I make absolutely no claim to be a composer in any shape or form. This piece was written mostly for the amusement of my son and myself. It consists of a melody I wrote when I was about 12 years old, and some strange noises that will annoy any long-suffering teacher or parent. I recommend that it is played after the proper pieces in this book have been practised, as a way of winding down (or up, in the case of said teacher or parent). The narrator can be the cellist, the cellist and the pianist, or a friend bamboozled into it.
A quote	'A bit of (hopefully harmless) fun'
Two favourite books	*Armadale*, Wilkie Collins *The Land of Green Ginger*, Noel Langley

Elegy

Carl Davis

for Steven Isserlis
Album leaf, Op. 66

Lowell Liebermann

Andante piacevole, con molto rubato (♩ = *c*.88)

to Gabriel Isserlis

Frogs dancing on water lilies

Olli Mustonen

Cantilena

John Woolrich

for Steven Isserlis

Hip hip bourrée

Julian Jacobson

for Steven Isserlis

Vocalise

Mark-Anthony Turnage

Tango flageoletto

David Matthews

to Gabriel – of course!

The haunted house

Steven Isserlis

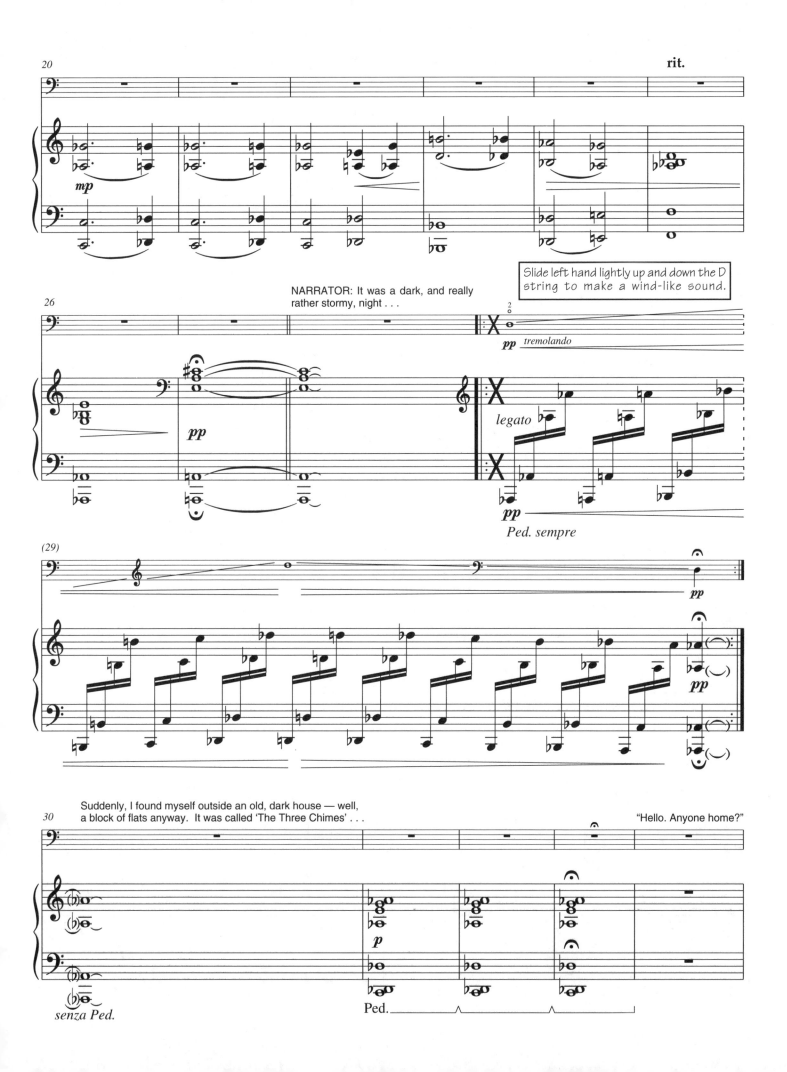

NARRATOR: It was a dark, and really
rather stormy, night . . .

Slide left hand lightly up and down the D
string to make a wind-like sound.

Suddenly, I found myself outside an old, dark house — well,
a block of flats anyway. It was called 'The Three Chimes' . . .

"Hello. Anyone home?"

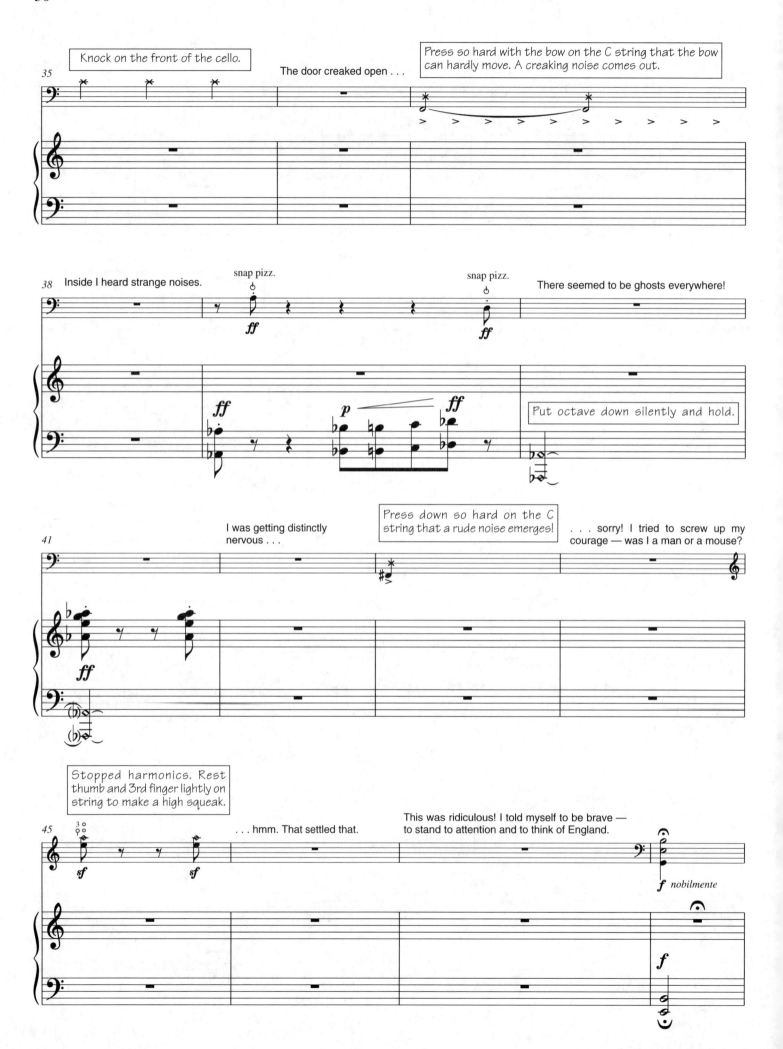

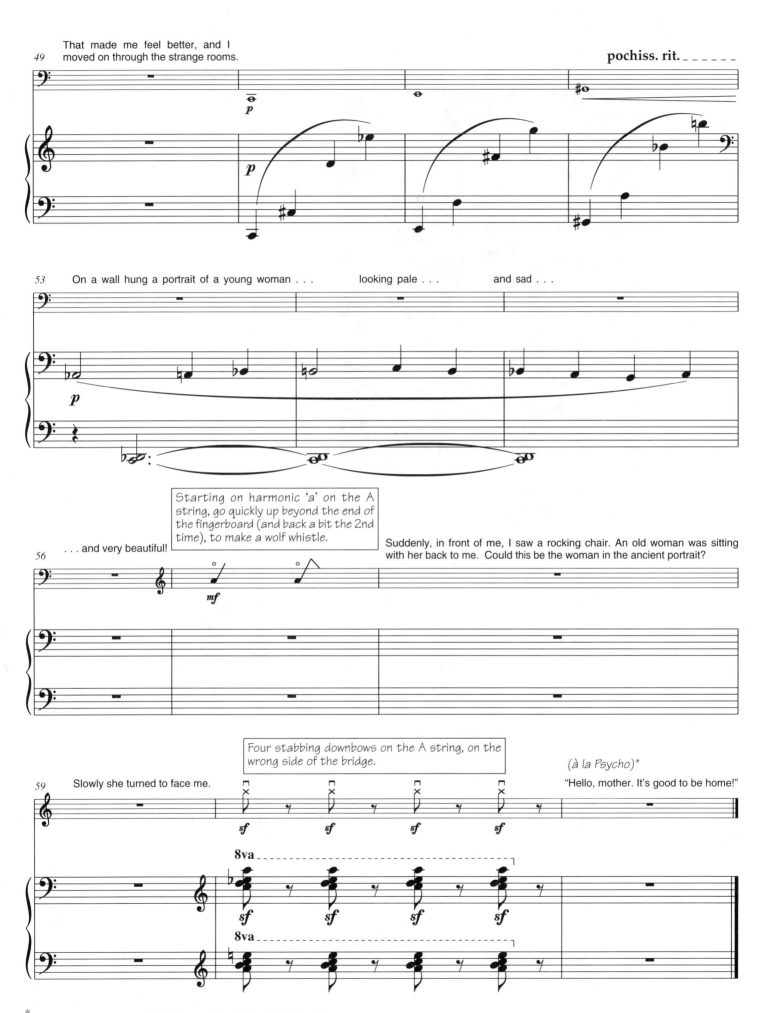

That made me feel better, and I moved on through the strange rooms.

pochiss. rit. _ _ _ _ _ _

On a wall hung a portrait of a young woman . . .   looking pale . . .   and sad . . .

Starting on harmonic 'a' on the A string, go quickly up beyond the end of the fingerboard (and back a bit the 2nd time), to make a wolf whistle.

. . . and very beautiful!

Suddenly, in front of me, I saw a rocking chair. An old woman was sitting with her back to me. Could this be the woman in the ancient portrait?

Four stabbing downbows on the A string, on the wrong side of the bridge.

(à la Psycho)*

Slowly she turned to face me.   "Hello, mother. It's good to be home!"

* A wonderfully creepy film directed by Alfred Hitchcock.

Steven Isserlis's
Cello World

HUBERT LÉONARD
The Donkey and the Driver

GABRIEL FAURÉ
Morceau de concours

SERGEI RACHMANINOV
Lied

ALEXANDER SCRIABIN
Romance

ANTONÍN DVOŘÁK
Romantic Piece

JULIUS ISSERLIS
Souvenir russe

ROBERT SCHUMANN
Intermezzo

SULKHAN TSINTSADZE
Chonguri

DAVID POPPER
Elfentanz

HEITOR VILLA-LOBOS
Song of the Black Swan

ISBN 0-571-51885-0

The cello as singer, as dancer, as folk instrument, even as donkey!

Cello World is a must for all cellists, a wonderful collection of original works and arrangements from the repertoire of world-famous cellist Steven Isserlis. The inspired line up of pieces includes Schumann's moving *Intermezzo*, Léonard's hysterical *The Donkey and the Driver* and Villa-Lobos' rippling *Song of the Black Swan*.

The music in this volume is recorded by Steven Isserlis with Thomas Adès (piano) on the BMG recording *Cello World* 09026 68928 2.

Also available from Faber Music:

Ludwig van Beethoven *Andante con Variazioni*	ISBN 0-571-51114-7
Ferruccio Busoni *Serenata, Op.34*	ISBN 0-571-51853-2
Ernest Chausson *Pièce, Op.39*	ISBN 0-571-51647-5
Camille Saint-Saëns *The Complete Shorter Works for Cello and Piano*	ISBN 0-571-51807-9
Carl Vine *Inner World*	ISBN 0-571-51748-X

Letts
gets you through

GW00645388

KS2 MATHS

SATs SUCCESS

PRACTICE TEST PAPERS

Ages 10–11

KS2 MATHS SATs

2 complete tests

PRACTICE TEST PAPERS

TOM HALL

Contents

ACKNOWLEDGEMENTS

The author and publisher are grateful to the copyright holders for permission to use quoted materials and images.

All other images are © Shutterstock.com

Every effort has been made to trace copyright holders and obtain their permission for the use of copyright material. The author and publisher will gladly receive information enabling them to rectify any error or omission in subsequent editions. All facts are correct at time of going to press.

Published by Letts Educational
An imprint of HarperCollins*Publishers* Ltd
1 London Bridge Street
London SE1 9GF

ISBN: 978-0-00-830054-8

First published 2018

10 9 8 7 6 5 4 3 2

Text, Design and Illustration
© Letts Educational, an imprint of HarperCollins*Publishers* Ltd 2018

All rights reserved. No part of this publication may be reproduced, stored in a retrieval system, or transmitted, in any form or by any means, electronic, mechanical, photocopying, recording or otherwise, without the prior permission of Letts Educational.

British Library Cataloguing in Publication Data.

A CIP record of this book is available from the British Library.

Series Concept and Development: Michelle I'Anson
Commissioning Editor: Alison James
Author: Tom Hall
Editorial: Rebecca Rothwell and Richard Toms
Cover Design: Amparo Barrera and Paul Oates
Inside Concept Design: Ian Wrigley
Text Design and Layout: Aptara®, Inc.
Artwork: Letts Educational and Aptara®, Inc.
Production: Lyndsey Rogers
Printed by CPI Group (UK) Ltd, Croydon, CR0 4YY

MIX
Paper from
responsible source
FSC™ C007454

This book is produced from independently certified FSC™ paper to ensure responsible forest management.

For more information visit:
www.harpercollins.co.uk/green

Introduction and instructions

Key Stage 2 SATs and how these practice test papers will help your child

The KS2 SATs are taken at the end of Year 6 (age 11). Here's a breakdown of the tests:

Maths	English reading	English grammar, punctuation and spelling
Paper 1: arithmetic (30 minutes) Paper 2: reasoning (40 minutes) Paper 3: reasoning (40 minutes)	Reading (1 hour)	Paper 1: questions (45 minutes) Paper 2: spelling (approximately 15 minutes)

This book is made up of two complete sets of maths practice test papers. Each set contains similar test papers to those that your child will take in maths at the end of Year 6. They can be used any time throughout the year to provide practice for the Key Stage 2 tests.

The results of the papers will give a good idea of your child's strengths and weaknesses.

Administering the tests

- Provide your child with a quiet environment where they can complete each test undisturbed.
- Provide a pen or pencil, ruler, eraser and protractor. A calculator is **not** allowed.
- The amount of time given for each paper varies, so remind your child at the start of each one how long they have and give them access to a clock or watch.
- You should only read the instructions out to your child, not the actual questions.
- Although handwriting is not assessed, remind your child that their answers should be clear.
- Advise your child that if they are unable to do one of the questions they should go on to the next one and come back to it later, if they have time. If they finish before the end, they should go back and check their work.

Paper 1: arithmetic

- Answers are worth 1 or 2 marks, with a total number of 40 marks. Long multiplication and long division questions are worth 2 marks each. A mark may be awarded for showing the correct method.
- Your child will have **30 minutes** to answer the questions as carefully as they can.
- Encourage your child to look at the number of marks after each question to help them find out how much detail is required in their answer.
- Where questions are expressed as common fractions, the answers should be given as common fractions. All other answers should be given as whole or decimal numbers.

Paper 2 and Paper 3: reasoning

- Answers are worth 1, 2 or 3 marks, with a total number of 35 marks. A mark may be awarded for showing the correct method in questions where there is a method box.
- Your child will have **40 minutes** to answer the questions as carefully as they can.
- Encourage your child to look at the number of marks after each question to help them find out how much detail is required in their answer.
- If your child needs to do some working out, they can use the space around the question.

Marking the practice test papers

The answers and mark scheme have been provided to enable you to check how your child has performed. Fill in the marks that your child achieved for each part of the tests.

Please note: these tests are **only a guide** to the standard or mark your child can achieve and cannot guarantee the same is achieved during the Key Stage 2 tests, as the mark needed to achieve the expected standard varies from year to year.

	Set A	**Set B**
Paper 1: arithmetic	/40	/40
Paper 2: reasoning	/35	/35
Paper 3: reasoning	/35	/35
Total	/110	/110

The scores achieved on these practice test papers will help to show if your child is working at the expected standard in maths:
35–57 = working towards the expected standard
58–94 = working at the expected standard
95–110 = working above the expected standard.

When an area of weakness has been identified, it is useful to go over it and to look at similar types of questions with your child. Sometimes your child will be familiar with the subject matter but might not understand what the question is asking. This will become apparent when talking to your child.

Shared marking and target setting

Engaging your child in the marking process will help them to develop a greater understanding of the tests and, more importantly, provide them with some ownership of their learning. They will be able to see more clearly how and why certain areas have been identified for them to target for improvement.

Top tips for your child

Don't make silly mistakes. Make sure you emphasise to your child the importance of reading the question. Easy marks can be picked up by just doing as the question asks.

Make answers clearly legible. If your child has made a mistake, encourage them to put a cross through it and write the correct answer clearly next to it. Try to encourage your child to use an eraser as little as possible.

Don't panic! These practice test papers, and indeed the end of Key Stage 2 tests, are meant to provide a guide to the standard a child has attained. They are not the be-all and end-all, as children are assessed regularly throughout the school year. Explain to your child that there is no need to worry if they cannot do a question – tell them to go on to the next question and come back to the problematic question later if they have time.

Key Stage 2

Maths

Paper 1: arithmetic

You **may not** use a calculator to answer any questions in this test paper.

Time:

You have **30 minutes** to complete this test paper.

Maximum mark	Actual mark
40	

First name	
Last name	

Date of birth	Day		Month		Year	

1

43 × 5 =

1 mark

2

574 + 56 =

1 mark

3

434 ÷ 1 =

1 mark

4

$\dfrac{2}{5} + \dfrac{2}{5} =$

1 mark

5

= 9,999 − 1,000

1 mark

6

10 × 6 × 3 =

1 mark

7 607 × 3 =

1 mark

8 8.1 ÷ 10 =

1 mark

9 316 + 86 =

1 mark

10 $5^2 =$

1 mark

11 $492 \div 3 =$

1 mark

12 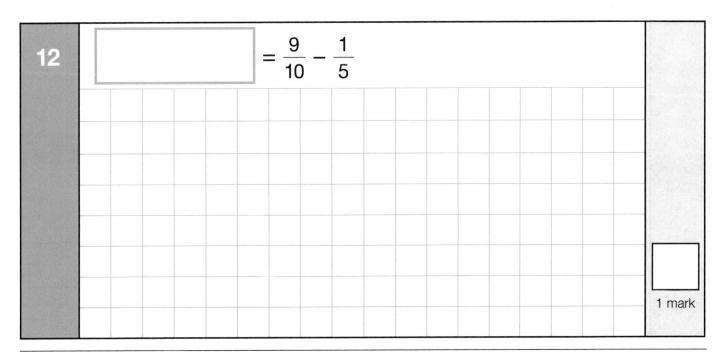 $= \dfrac{9}{10} - \dfrac{1}{5}$

1 mark

13

$320 \div 4 =$

1 mark

14

$\dfrac{1}{2} + \dfrac{2}{5} =$

1 mark

15

$\dfrac{1}{3}$ of 2,400 =

1 mark

16

$\dfrac{1}{2} \div 4 =$

1 mark

17

[   ] $= 0.6 \times 4$

1 mark

18

50% of 2,500 =

1 mark

19   50 − 5 × 10 =

20   5,725 − 375 =

21   5,804 − 507 =

22 $125 \div 25 =$

1 mark

23 $486.48 - 39.57 =$

1 mark

24

```
    2 3 4
×     2 6
```

Show your method

2 marks

25

```
2 3 | 5 5 2
```

Show your method

2 marks

26 30.75 × 100 =

1 mark

27 $\frac{3}{4} + \frac{4}{12} =$

1 mark

28 78.7 − 65.88 =

1 mark

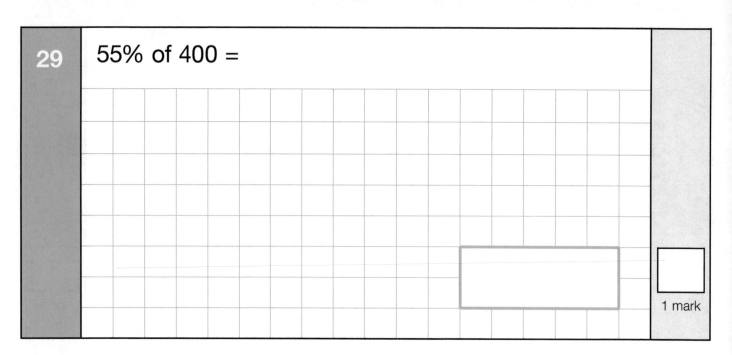

29 55% of 400 =

1 mark

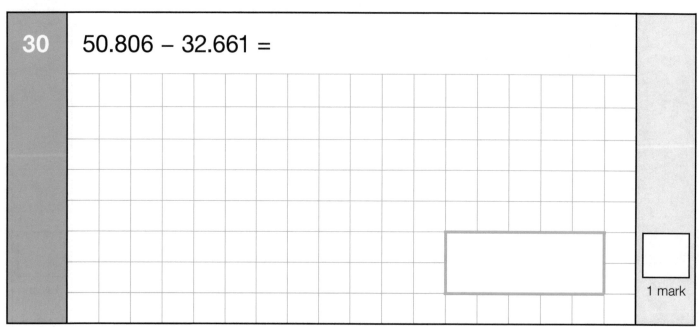

30 50.806 − 32.661 =

1 mark

31

$$
\begin{array}{r}
5\ 7\ 3 \\
\times\ \ \ 4\ 5 \\
\hline
\end{array}
$$

Show your method

2 marks

32

$\dfrac{3}{5} \div 4 =$

1 mark

33

3 5 | 7 8 7 5

Show your method

2 marks

34

$$4\frac{3}{4} + 5\frac{2}{5} =$$

1 mark

35

$$\frac{1}{3} \times \frac{1}{5} =$$

1 mark

36

56.77 − 5.777 =

1 mark

Key Stage 2

Maths

Paper 2: reasoning

You **may not** use a calculator to answer any questions in this test paper.

Time:

You have **40 minutes** to complete this test paper.

Maximum mark	Actual mark
35	....

First name	
Last name	

Date of birth	Day		Month		Year	

1 This is part of a number square.

Circle all the numbers that have a remainder of 1 when divided by 4.

12	13	14	15	16
22	23	24	25	26
32	33	34	35	36
42	43	44	45	46
52	53	54	55	56

2 marks

2 Draw a pentagon with a pair of parallel lines.

Use a ruler.

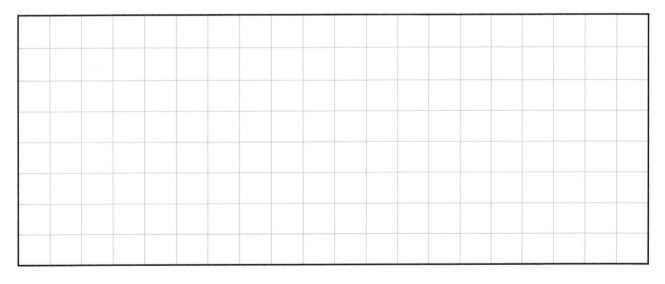

2 marks

3 Ellie and Rosie each buy one pizza.

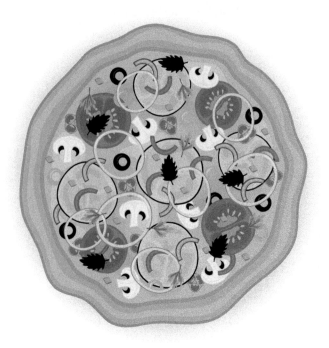 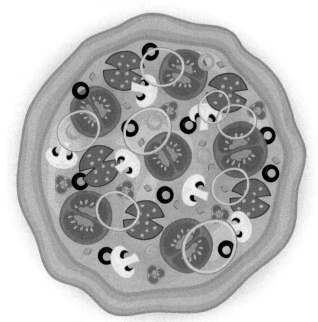

Ellie eats $\frac{5}{8}$ of her pizza.

Rosie eats $\frac{7}{8}$ of her pizza.

What fraction of one pizza is left?

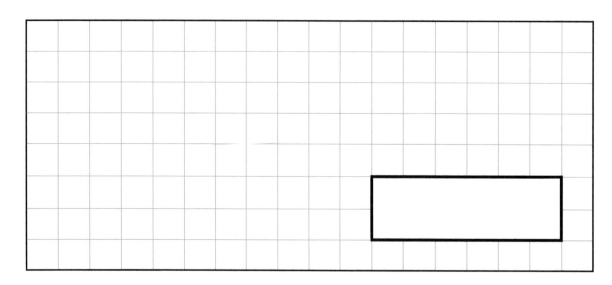

1 mark

4 Here are the temperatures in four cities at midnight and midday.

City	Temperature	
	At midnight	At midday
Athens	5°C	10°C
Berlin	–6°C	–1°C
Cairo	5°C	15°C
London	–3°C	4°C

At midnight, how many degrees colder is Berlin than Cairo?

°C

1 mark

Tick the cities that have a 5°C increase in temperature from midnight to midday.

Athens

Berlin

Cairo

London

1 mark

5 Write the missing digits in this calculation.

$$5 \quad \boxed{} \quad 4 \quad \boxed{}$$
$$+ \quad \boxed{} \quad 5 \quad \boxed{} \quad 4$$
$$\overline{}$$
$$1 \quad 2 \quad 6 \quad 0 \quad 0$$

1 mark

6 Calculate the perimeter of this shape.

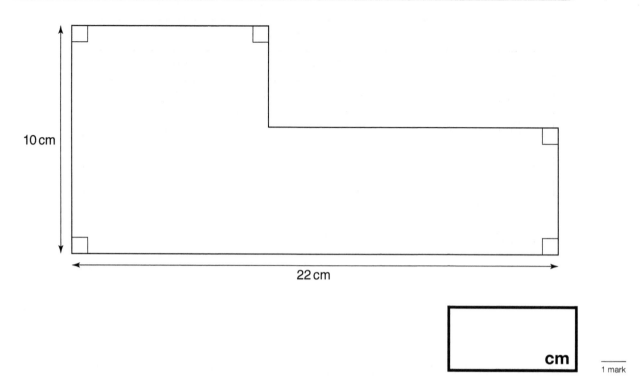

10 cm

22 cm

cm

7 A number squared and a number cubed both equal 64.

Find the numbers.

$\boxed{}^2 = 64 = \boxed{}^3$

8 Four hundred and sixty thousand, three hundred and five

Write this number in digits.

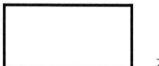

9 Reflect the shape in the mirror line.

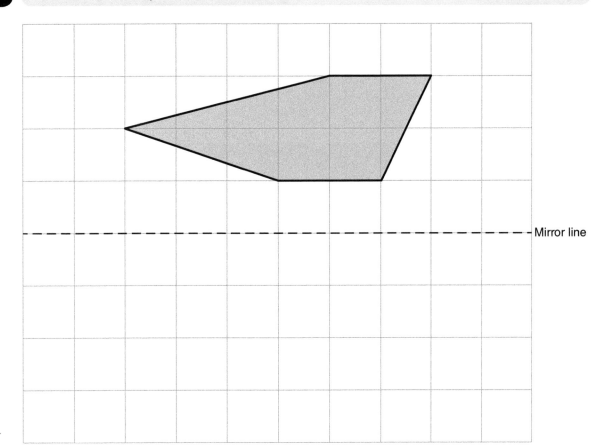

Mirror line

1 mark

10 This table gives approximate conversions between kilograms and pounds.

kilograms	pounds
1	2.2
2	4.4
4	8.8
8	17.6
16	35.2

Use the table to convert 7 kilograms into pounds.

pounds

1 mark

Use the table to convert 22 pounds into kilograms.

kg

1 mark

11 This is the plan of a football ground which has seats for 48,139 spectators.

The number of seats is shown for three of the stands.

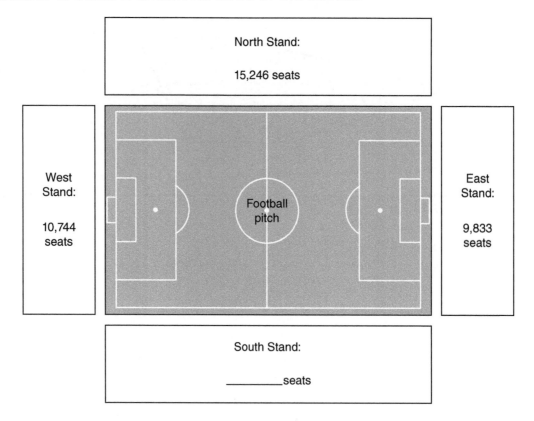

North Stand:

15,246 seats

West Stand:

10,744 seats

Football pitch

East Stand:

9,833 seats

South Stand:

_____seats

How many seats are there in the South Stand?

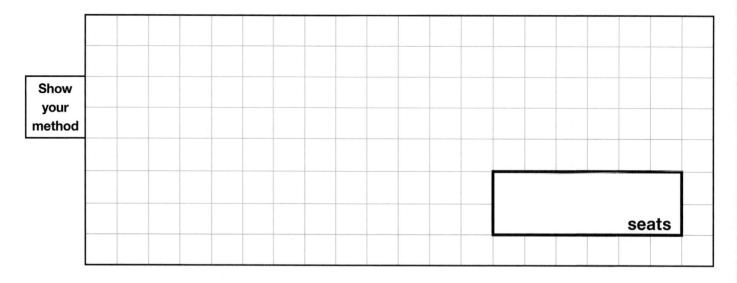

Show your method

seats

2 marks

12 There are 12 pencils in a box.

A pack holds 24 boxes.

A school buys 8 packs.

How many pencils does the school buy?

Show your method

pencils

2 marks

13 Tom has a collection of football cards.

Tom has 5 coloured cards to every 3 black and white cards.

He has 36 black and white cards.

Tom gives $\frac{1}{5}$ of his coloured cards to Jack.

How many cards does Tom give to Jack?

Show your method

cards

2 marks

14 $330 \div 8 =$

Give your answer as a decimal.

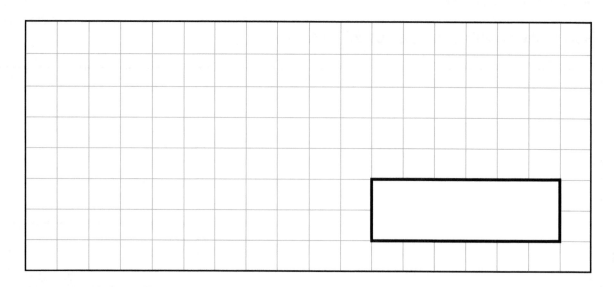

15 Oakview School has 460 pupils.

40% are girls.

Sea Lane School has 240 pupils.

60% are girls.

How many more girls are there at Oakview School?

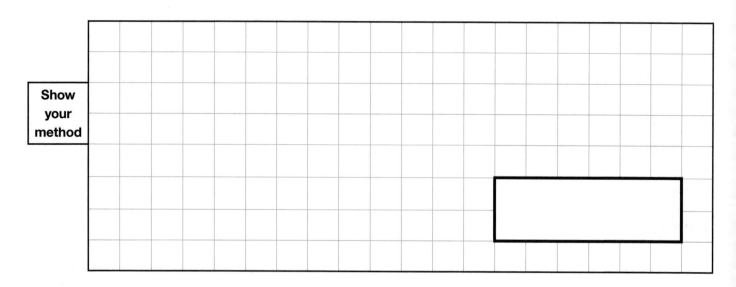

Show your method

16   Find the value of $5a - 2b$, when $a = 5$ and $b = 7$.

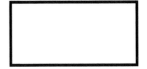

1 mark

Find the value of $5a + 2b$, when $a = 7$ and $b = 5$.

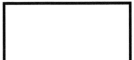

1 mark

17   Here are two equations with missing numbers.

$$\square + \triangle = 18$$

$$\square - \triangle = 6$$

Work out the value of the missing numbers.

$$\square = \boxed{}$$

$$\triangle = \boxed{}$$

1 mark

18 Here are four containers holding some water.

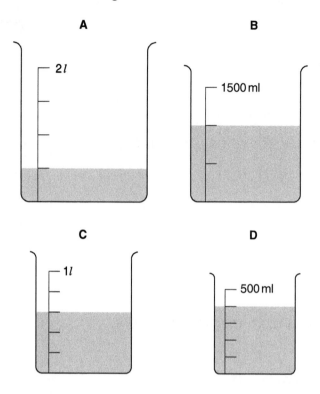

Which container is holding the **most** water?

1 mark

What is the **difference** in the amount of water in container **A** and container **C**?

1 mark

19 A square is drawn so that it joins an equilateral triangle:

What is the size of angle A?

°

1 mark

20 Here is a set of numbers.

| 7 | 15 | 24 | 30 | 48 | 53 |

Which two numbers are **common multiples** of 3 and 4?

	and	

1 mark

Which two numbers are **common factors** of 60?

	and	

1 mark

Which two numbers are **prime numbers**?

	and	

1 mark

21 Sally wants to go on holiday to Spain.

She compares the mean temperatures for UK and Spain.

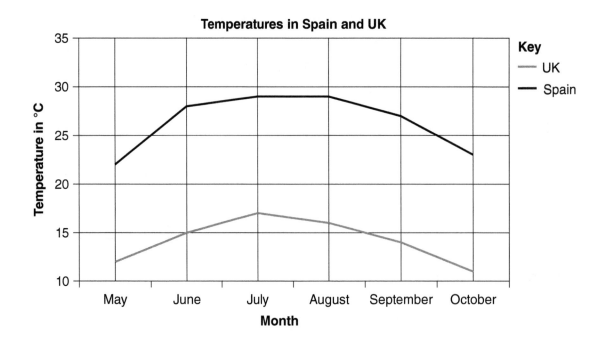

How much **warmer** was it in Spain than in UK in September?

°C

1 mark

Sally wants to go to Spain when it is closest to 25°C.

Which **two** months could Sally choose?

_____

1 mark

Key Stage 2

Maths

Paper 3: reasoning

You **may not** use a calculator to answer any questions in this test paper.

Time:

You have **40 minutes** to complete this test paper.

Maximum mark	Actual mark
35	

First name	
Last name	

Date of birth	Day		Month		Year	

1 Jess has put beads on this abacus to make a number:

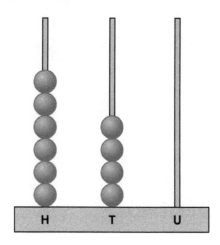

What number could Jess make if she adds one more bead?

1 mark

2 Find the missing number.

$9 \times \boxed{} = 72 \div 2$

1 mark

3 Dev sets his alarm for the time shown on the clock.

At what time will his alarm go off?

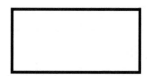

1 mark

4 Part of this shape is missing.

The dotted line is a line of symmetry.

Complete the shape.

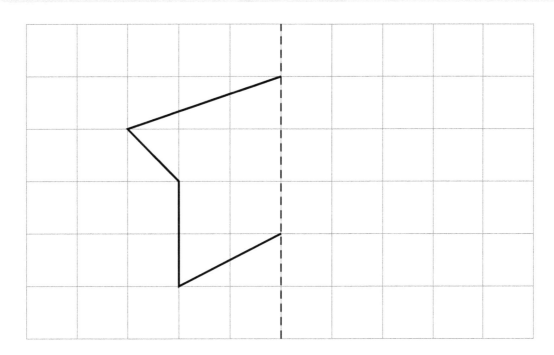

1 mark

Draw the line of symmetry on this shape.

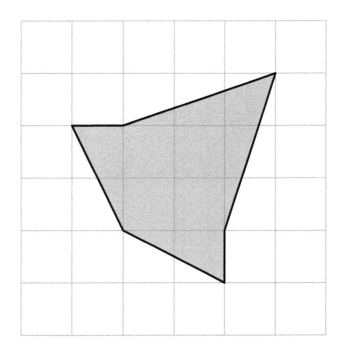

1 mark

5 Chloe has 217 minutes left on her phone.

She uses 83 minutes.

She gets another 350 minutes.

How many minutes does Chloe have on her phone now?

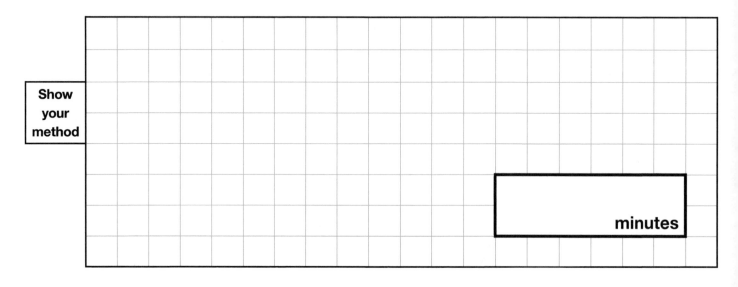

Show your method

minutes

2 marks

6 Tom buys 5 identical books for a total of £26.

What is the cost of each book?

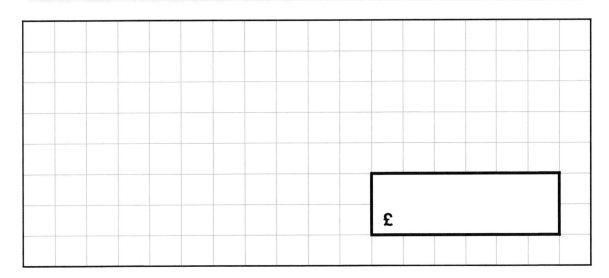

£

1 mark

7 1 inch is about 2.5 centimetres.

How many centimetres is 12 inches?

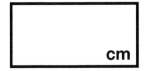

cm

1 mark

There are 12 inches in 1 foot.

There are 3 feet in 1 yard.

Is 1 yard shorter or longer than 1 metre? Explain how you know.

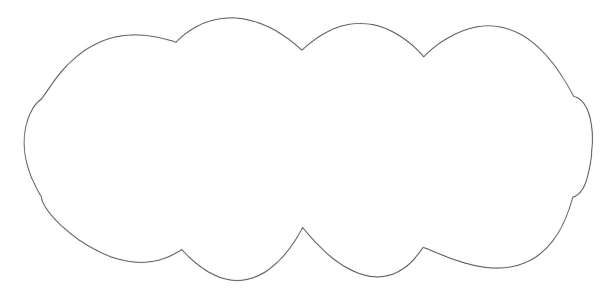

1 mark

8 The temperature outside a greenhouse is −4°C.

The temperature inside the greenhouse is 4°C.

What is the **difference** between the two temperatures?

°C

1 mark

9 Two prime numbers total 31.

What are the two numbers?

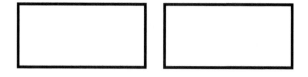

1 mark

List the prime numbers that are greater than 40 and less than 50.

 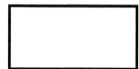

1 mark

10 Manisha has 24 counters.

- $\frac{1}{4}$ of the counters are red.

- $\frac{1}{3}$ of the counters are blue.

- $\frac{3}{8}$ of the counters are green.

The rest of the counters are yellow.

How many yellow counters are there?

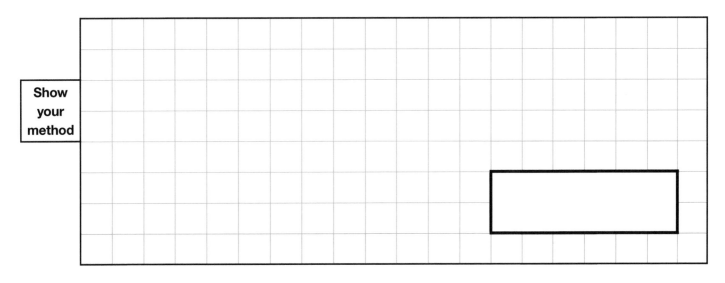

Show
your
method

2 marks

11 878,421 − 319,875 =

Pavel wants to complete this calculation. First, he wants to estimate his answer.

He rounds each number to the nearest hundred thousand and subtracts the rounded numbers.

What is Pavel's estimated answer?

1 mark

12 Harvey has seven digit cards:

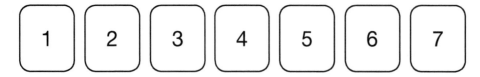

Harvey arranges all seven digit cards to make a number.

Harvey's number has:

- five million

- thirty thousand

- seven hundred

What is the largest number Harvey can make?

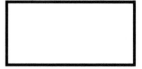

1 mark

Next, Harvey uses **five** of the cards to make the number nearest to fifty thousand.

Write the number Harvey makes.

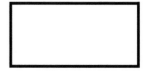

1 mark

13   Measure the marked angle using a protractor.

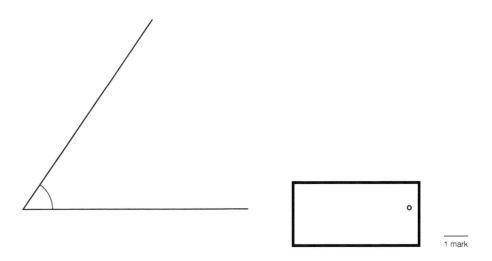

°

14   The population of a city is 275,386.

- 54,895 are aged 65 and over.

- 143,706 are aged 18 to 64.

How many are aged under 18?

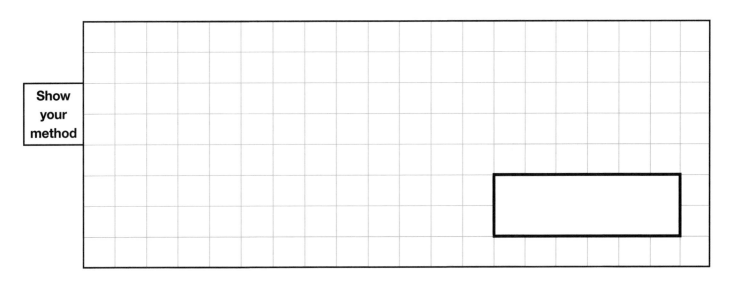

Show your method

15 This is a diagram of Jen's garden. It shows the fractions of the garden Jen has planted with flowers and grass.

Flowers $\frac{1}{4}$	
Patio	Grass $\frac{3}{5}$

The remaining area is a patio.

What **fraction** of the garden is the patio?

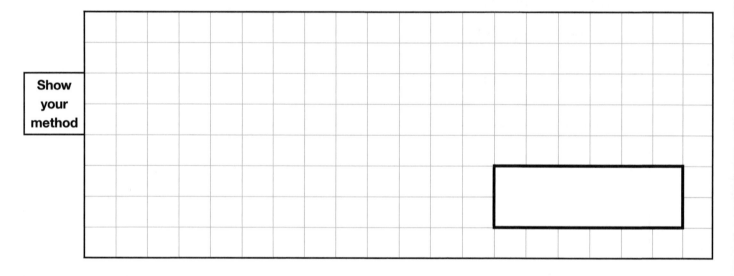

Show your method

_____
2 marks

16 Write these masses in order, **heaviest** first.

2.5 kg   200 g   2.05 kg   2,550 g   2.005 kg

_____
1 mark

17

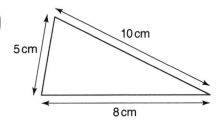

Serena draws a **similar** triangle:

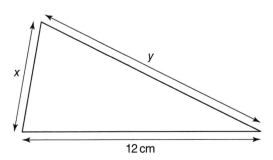

What are the missing lengths of Serena's triangle?

$x =$ [ ] cm

1 mark

$y =$ [ ] cm

1 mark

18 There 30 pupils in a class.

The teacher has 12 litres of orange juice.

She pours 350 ml of orange juice for every pupil.

How much orange juice is left over?

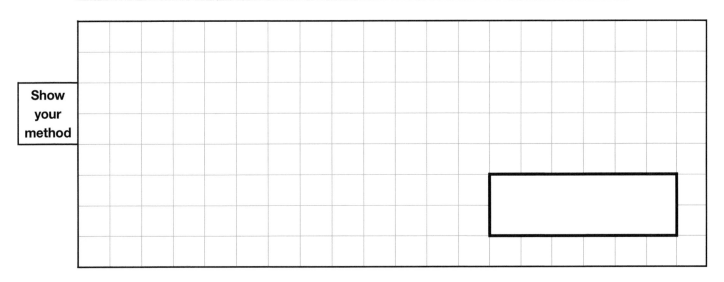

Show your method

3 marks

19 Teachers asked 120 children where they would like to go on a school visit.

This pie chart shows where they chose to go.

School visit

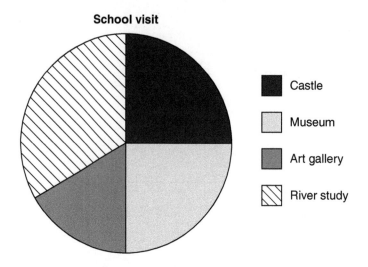

■ Castle

□ Museum

▨ Art gallery

▧ River study

Estimate how many children chose to visit the castle.

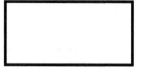

1 mark

40 children chose the river study.

What size angle at the centre of the pie chart is needed to show the river study?

°

1 mark

Half the children chose either the river study or the art gallery.

How many children chose to visit the art gallery?

1 mark

20 Abi sat 6 tests.

Her mean score was 45.

How many marks did Abi score **altogether**?

21 A formula to find the perimeter, *P*, of a rectangle is

> *P* = 2*l* + 2*w*, where *l* = length and *w* = width

Work out the length of a rectangle that has a perimeter of 80 cm and a width of 10 cm.

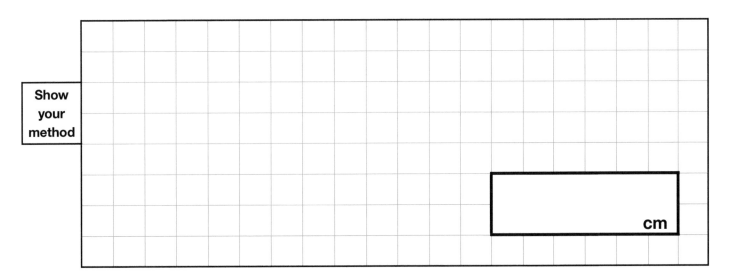

Show your method

cm

Key Stage 2

Maths

Paper 1: arithmetic

You **may not** use a calculator to answer any questions in this test paper.

Time:

You have **30 minutes** to complete this test paper.

Maximum mark	Actual mark
40	....

First name	
Last name	

Date of birth	Day		Month		Year	

1

$40 \div 5 =$

1 mark

2

$4,828 - 83 =$

1 mark

3

$\dfrac{7}{8} - \dfrac{4}{8} =$

1 mark

4 $\dfrac{1}{2} \times 30 =$

1 mark

5 [ ] $= 888 + 1,000$

1 mark

6 $855 + 477 =$

1 mark

7   765 ÷ 5 =

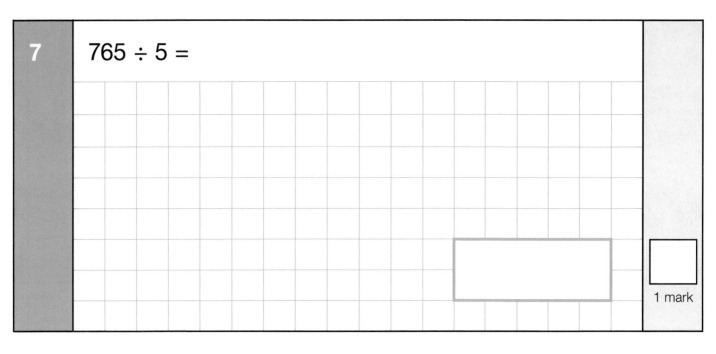

1 mark

8   0.6 × 100 =

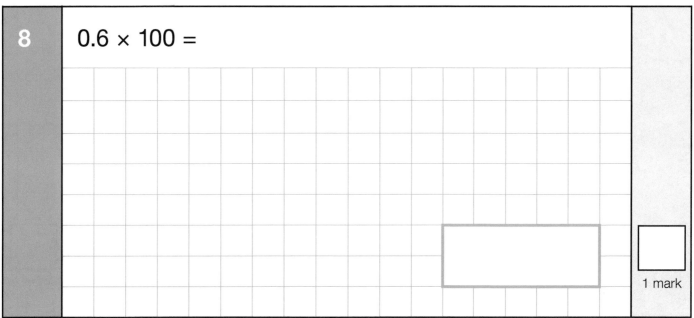

1 mark

9   ⬚ = 4,715 − 808

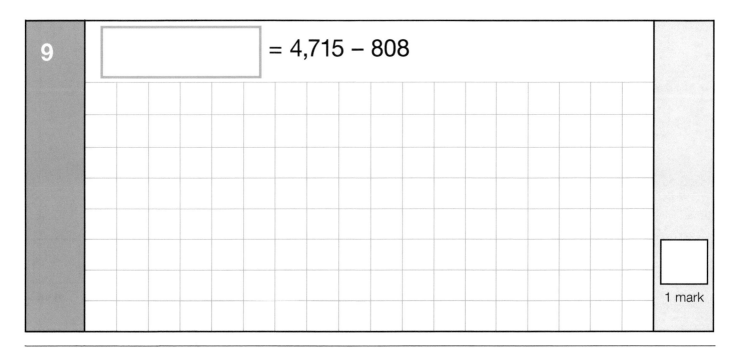

1 mark

10

$\boxed{} = 3^3$

1 mark

11

$4{,}088 \times 6 =$

$\boxed{}$

1 mark

12

$6{,}000{,}000 + \boxed{} + 7 = 6{,}090{,}007$

1 mark

13 0.03 × 6 =

1 mark

14 $\frac{1}{2} - \frac{1}{10} =$

1 mark

15 0.3 × 18 =

1 mark

16

[   ] = 325.8 + 4.67

1 mark

17 80,000 − 8,000 =

1 mark

18 $\dfrac{1}{10} \div 2 =$

1 mark

19 9,360 − 745 =

1 mark

20 23.9 + 4.76 =

1 mark

21 $5\frac{3}{4} - \frac{3}{8} =$

1 mark

22	20 × 30 × 40 =	
		1 mark

23	30% of 3,000 =	
		1 mark

24	75 ÷ 1,000 =	
		1 mark

25 654.23 − 40.8 =

1 mark

26

```
    1 8 2
×     6 2
```

Show your method

2 marks

27 $100 \times 2\frac{1}{2} =$

1 mark

28

$22 \overline{\smash{)}704}$

Show your method

2 marks

29 $40 + 10 \times 2 =$

1 mark

30

Show your method

$$7 \, 1 \,\big|\, 1 \; 4 \; 9 \; 1$$

2 marks

31

$$4\frac{2}{3} - 3\frac{3}{5} =$$

1 mark

32

Show your method

```
    3 0 7 4
  ×     3 5
```

2 marks

© 2018 Letts Educational, an imprint of HarperCollinsPublishers Ltd – not to be photocopied.

33   4,000,000 – 400,000 =

1 mark

34   78.357 – 6.05 =

1 mark

35 $\dfrac{3}{5} \times 40 =$

1 mark

36 $\dfrac{2}{3} \div 2 =$

1 mark

Key Stage 2

Maths

Paper 2: reasoning

You **may not** use a calculator to answer any questions in this test paper.

Time:

You have **40 minutes** to complete this test paper.

Maximum mark	Actual mark
35	....

First name	
Last name	
Date of birth	Day		Month		Year	

1 Tick (✔) the right angles in this shape.

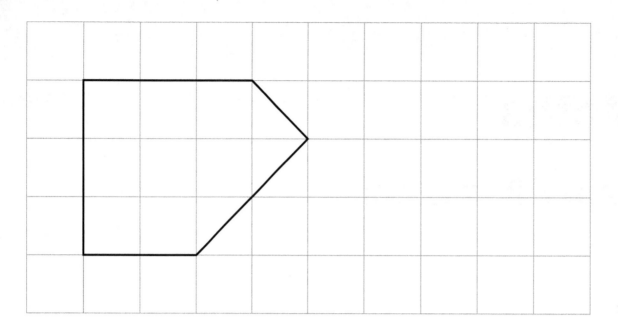

1 mark

2 Hartvale School played Sunnywood School in a football match.

Five goals were scored in the match.

Here is a list of the possible scores:

Hartvale School	5	:	0	Sunnywood School
Hartvale School	1	:	4	Sunnywood School
Hartvale School	0	:	5	Sunnywood School
Hartvale School	4	:	1	Sunnywood School
Hartvale School		:		Sunnywood School
Hartvale School		:		Sunnywood School

Write the two missing scores in the table.

1 mark

3 Dev read 26 books in a school year.

He drew a graph to show how many books he read each term.

Complete the bar for Term 3.

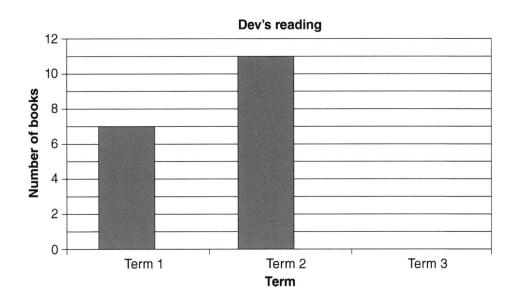

4 A train has 8 coaches.

Each coach has 72 seats.

The ticket collector says, 'I know 70 × 8 = 560'

What must he add to 560 to find how many seats there are in the train **altogether**?

5 A machine packs biscuits.

Each packet holds 8 biscuits.

The machine packs 900 biscuits.

How many packets will be filled using the 900 biscuits?

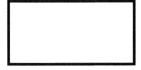

packets

6 A square is drawn on an empty grid.

The coordinates of three vertices are marked.

What are the coordinates of the fourth vertex?

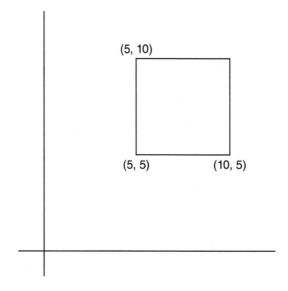

(5, 10)

(5, 5)   (10, 5)

$$\left(\underline{\quad}, \underline{\quad}\right)$$

1 mark

7 A shop has a special offer.

Special offer!

Buy 3 tins of soup and get 1 free

Obi pays for 12 tins of soup.

How many tins does Obi get?

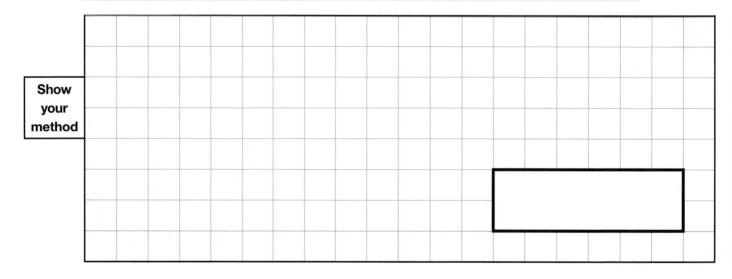

Show your method

2 marks

8 Max makes some concrete for a path.

For a path 8 metres long Max needs:

- 200 kg of cement

- 600 kg of sand

- 600 kg of stone

What weight of stone will he need for a path 20 metres long?

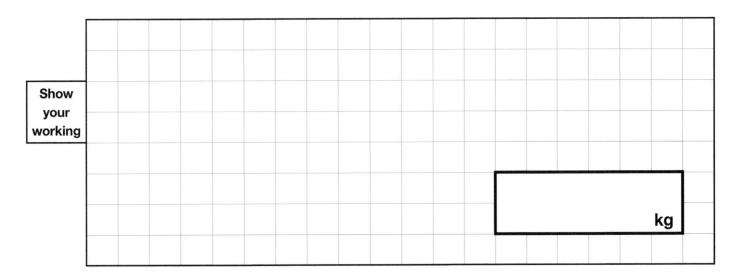

Show your working

kg

2 marks

9 Calculate the missing number.

$$56 \times 9 = \boxed{} + 4$$

1 mark

Calculate the missing number.

$$56 + 64 = 3 \times 4 \times \boxed{}$$

2 marks

10 Here are some digit cards.

| 4 | 4 | 5 | 5 | 6 | 6 |

Use the digit cards to complete this equation.

Use each card only once.

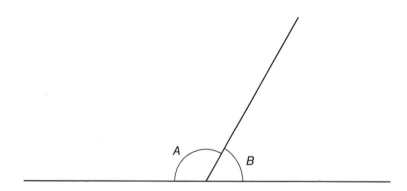

1 mark

11

What is the **total** of angle A and angle B?

$$\boxed{} \; ^\circ$$

1 mark

66   © 2018 Letts Educational, an imprint of HarperCollinsPublishers Ltd – not to be photocopied.

12 Josh wants to buy tickets for a concert.

He needs 9 adult tickets and 3 child tickets.

CONCERT

Tickets

Adult: £24.70

Child: £18.50

Group of 12: £249.99

How much will Josh save if he buys the group ticket?

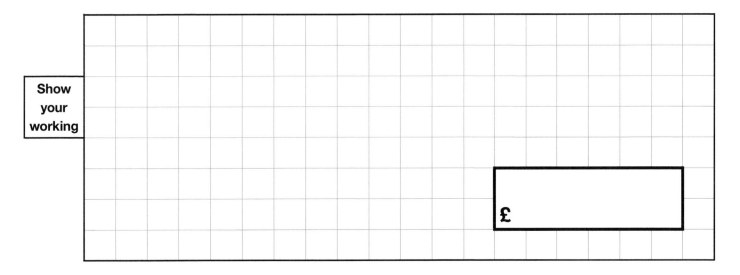

Show your working

£

3 marks

13 Here are two fair triangular spinners.

Each spinner is spun once and the numbers added to give a total.

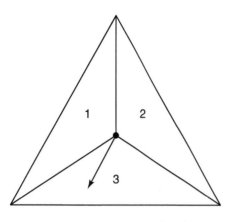 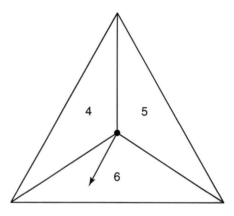

List the totals that can be made.

 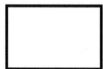 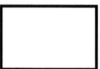 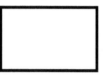 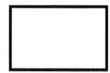

2 marks

14 This sequence decreases in equal steps.

Find the missing numbers.

| 6 | −3 | | | −30 |

2 marks

15 Josef is thinking of a six-digit number.

Josef's number has:

- three hundred thousand

- seven hundred

- forty thousand

All the other digits are 6.

Use these facts to complete the number.

$$\boxed{}\ \boxed{}\ \boxed{}\ ,\ \boxed{}\ \boxed{}\ \boxed{}$$

1 mark

16 This table shows the temperatures in five cities.

City	London	Belfast	Manchester	Cardiff	Glasgow
Temperature	4°C	0°C	–3°C	–1°C	–5°C

What is the **difference** between the temperatures in Manchester and Cardiff?

°C

1 mark

What is the **difference** between the warmest and coldest temperatures?

°C

1 mark

17 A coach company works out the cost of hiring a coach by using this formula:

Cost = (£8 × number of passengers) + (£0.75 × number of miles)

A school is organising a coach trip for 30 children and 5 adults.

They will travel 80 miles.

How much will the coach company charge the school?

Show your method

£

2 marks

18 What could the missing digits be?

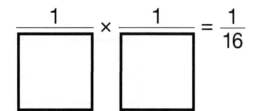

$$\frac{1}{\boxed{}} \times \frac{1}{\boxed{}} = \frac{1}{16}$$

1 mark

19 Dev and Sam share £45.

Dev takes half the amount Sam takes.

How much do they each take?

Dev takes  £

Sam takes £

1 mark

20 This rectangle has an area of 24 cm².

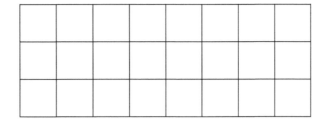

Write the lengths and widths of two different rectangles that also have an area of 24 cm².

length [   ] cm and width [   ] cm

1 mark

length [   ] cm and width [   ] cm

1 mark

21 Angles *x* and *y* are equal.

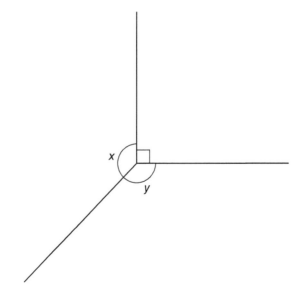

Calculate angle *x*.

X = [   ] °

1 mark

22 Ben describes two shapes.

Name each shape.

My first shape has four
right angles and two pairs
of sides of 10 cm and 5 cm.

My second shape has four
angles (two that are 120° and
two that are 60°) and two pairs
of sides that are 10 cm and 5 cm.

23 The shaded face of this cuboid has an area of 160 cm².

The width is 12 cm and the height is 8 cm.

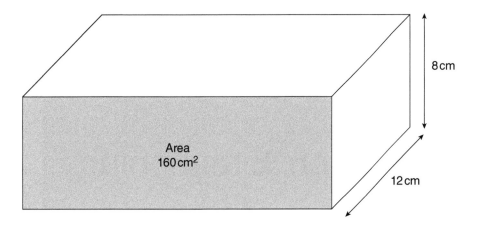

What is the volume of the cuboid?

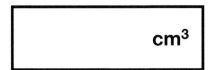

cm³

Key Stage 2

Maths

Paper 3: reasoning

You **may not** use a calculator to answer any questions in this test paper.

Time:

You have **40 minutes** to complete this test paper.

Maximum mark	Actual mark
35	....

First name	
Last name	

Date of birth	Day		Month		Year	

1 Yasmin completes a calculation using these digit cards:

| 3 | 4 | 5 | 6 | 7 |

She uses each card once.

Use the cards to show Yasmin's correct calculation.

+		
6	0	1

2 marks

2 This is a rectangle.

Tick (✔) **two** correct statements.

The two bold lines are perpendicular. ☐

The bold and thin lines are perpendicular. ☐

The two bold lines are parallel. ☐

The bold and thin lines are parallel. ☐

2 marks

3 Dom sells computer games.

This pictogram shows the number of computer games he sold one week.

Computer Game Sales

Sunday	⊙ ⊙ ⊙ ⊙
Monday	⊙ ◖
Tuesday	⊙ ◔
Wednesday	⊙
Thursday	⊙ ⊙ ⊙
Friday	⊙ ⊙ ⊙ ◝
Saturday	⊙ ⊙ ⊙ ⊙

⊙ stands for four computer games

How many computer games did Dom sell in total on Friday and Saturday?

games

1 mark

How many more games did Dom sell on Sunday than on Monday?

games

1 mark

4 Here are some trays of chocolates. Some of the chocolates in each tray have been eaten. A chocolate is shown by this symbol: ▢

Tick (✔) the trays that have $\frac{3}{4}$ of the chocolates **left**.

2 marks

5 Ned has a 10 kg bag of potatoes.

He uses 2.3 kg of the potatoes one day.

He uses 1,600 g of the potatoes on the next day.

What is the weight of potatoes left?

Show
your
working

2 marks

6 Translate the shape 7 squares right and 3 squares down.

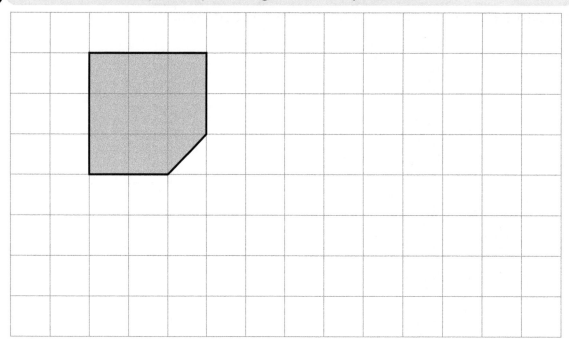

2 marks

7 There are two series on television.

The first series shows the year MMIX at the end of each programme.

The second series shows the year MMVII at the end of each programme.

How many years are there between each series?

years

1 mark

8 Circle the number that is both:

- a factor of 36

- a multiple of 12

9   18   24   36   72

1 mark

9 A bag contains 3.5 kg of lawn feed.

The instructions say that every square metre needs 50 grams of lawn feed.

How many square metres will the bag cover?

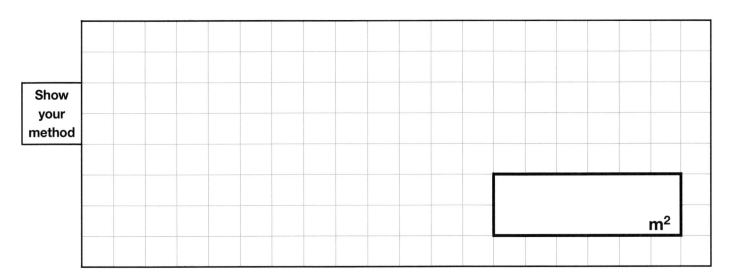

Show your method

m²

2 marks

10 There are 800 counters in a jar.

$\frac{4}{5}$ of the counters are **not** red.

How many counters are red?

Show your method

counters

2 marks

11 Here are three digit cards.

| 1 | | 2 | | 3 |

Use each card to complete the missing digits in these sentences.

Use each card only once.

   is a prime number.

   is a common multiple of 3 and 7.

   is a common factor of 62 and 93.

2 marks

12 Tara thinks of a number, n.

She adds 12 to the number and then multiplies the answer by 3.

Tick (✔) the expression that shows this.

$3n + 12$ ☐

$3(n + 12)$ ☐

$3 \times 12 \times n$ ☐

$36 + n$ ☐

$n(3 + 12)$ ☐

1 mark

13 Javid plays a computer game with **six levels**.

He can score 2,500 points at each level.

After Javid has played the game at three levels, he has scored 5,450 points.

After **all** six levels, what is the greatest number of points Javid could score?

Show your method																

points

2 marks

14 An aeroplane is flying at a height of 8,000 m.

The outside temperature is −45°C.

Inside the aeroplane the temperature is 18°C.

What is the **difference** between the two temperatures?

°C

1 mark

15 Sam sat two maths tests.

These were his scores:

Paper 1: $\dfrac{14}{20}$

Paper 2: $\dfrac{18}{25}$

Change Sam's fraction scores to percentage scores.

Paper 1: ☐ %

1 mark

Paper 2: ☐ %

1 mark

16 This pie chart shows the sports chosen by 80 children.

Here are some facts about the pie chart:

- 30 children chose tennis.

- The same number of children chose gymnastics as chose rugby.

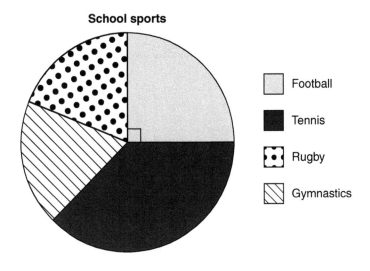

How many children chose rugby?

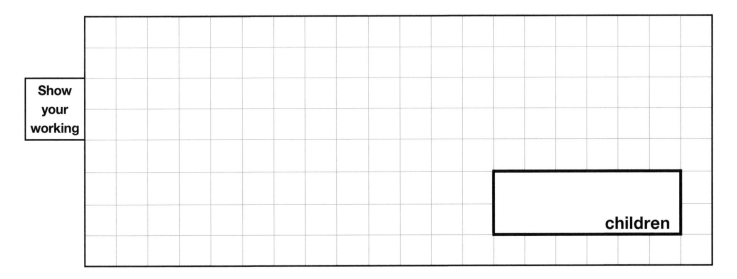

Show your working

children

2 marks

17 Kylie makes a series of patterns.

She gives each pattern a value.

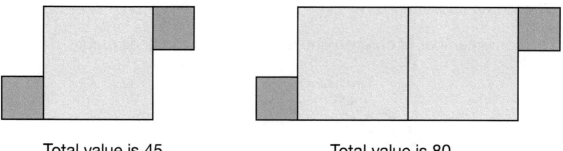

Total value is 45   Total value is 80

Calculate the value of this pattern.

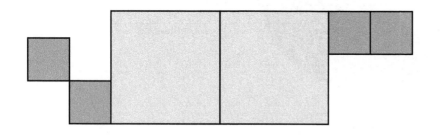

Show your method													

2 marks

18   Work out the area of this triangle.

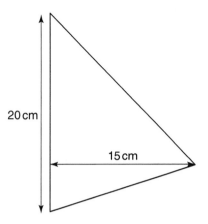

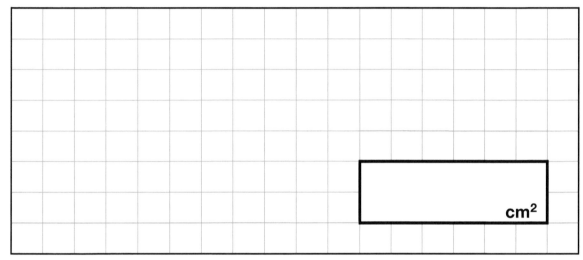

cm²

1 mark

19 The dots, A to F, can be joined to make a straight line.

The dots are drawn at regular intervals.

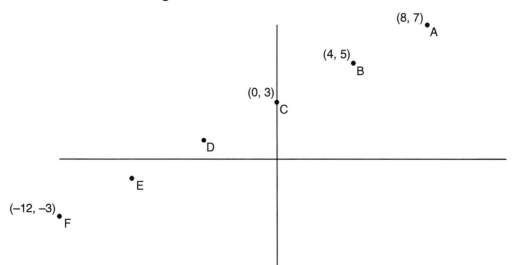

Some dots have coordinates.

What are the coordinates of dots D and E?

D = (—4— , —1—)

1 mark

E = (—8— , —1—)

1 mark

20 Tickets to an amusement park cost £17.50 each.

There is a special offer. Eight tickets can be bought for £110.

How much cheaper is **each** ticket with the special offer?

Show
your
method

£

2 marks

THIS PAGE HAS INTENTIONALLY BEEN LEFT BLANK

Answers

Set A Paper 1

1. 215   **(1 mark)**
2. 630   **(1 mark)**
3. 434   **(1 mark)**
4. $\frac{4}{5}$ (Accept equivalent fractions)   **(1 mark)**
5. 8,999   **(1 mark)**
6. 180   **(1 mark)**
7. 1,821   **(1 mark)**
8. 0.81   **(1 mark)**
9. 402   **(1 mark)**
10. 25   **(1 mark)**
11. 164   **(1 mark)**
12. $\frac{7}{10}$ (Accept equivalent fractions)   **(1 mark)**
13. 80   **(1 mark)**
14. $\frac{9}{10}$ (Accept equivalent fractions)   **(1 mark)**
15. 800   **(1 mark)**
16. $\frac{1}{8}$ (Accept equivalent fractions)   **(1 mark)**
17. 2.4   **(1 mark)**
18. 1,250   **(1 mark)**
19. 0   **(1 mark)**
20. 5,350   **(1 mark)**
21. 5,297   **(1 mark)**
22. 5   **(1 mark)**
23. 446.91   **(1 mark)**

24.

```
      2 3 4
  ×     2 6
  1 4 0 4
  4 6 8 0
  6 0 8 4
```

(2 marks for correct answer. Award 1 mark for using long multiplication with no more than one error but wrong answer given. Do not award any marks if the 0 for multiplying by a ten is missing. Do not award any marks if no final answer is given.)

25.

```
          2 4
  2 3 ) 5 5 2
        4 6
          9 2
          9 2
            0
```

(2 marks for correct answer. Award 1 mark for using long division with no more than one error but wrong answer given. Do not award any marks if no final answer is given.)

26. 3,075   **(1 mark)**
27. $1\frac{1}{12}$ (Accept equivalent fractions)   **(1 mark)**
28. 12.82   **(1 mark)**
29. 220   **(1 mark)**
30. 18.145   **(1 mark)**

31.

```
        5 7 3
  ×       4 5
    2 8 6 5
  2 2 9 2 0
  2 5 7 8 5
```

(2 marks for correct answer. Award 1 mark for using long multiplication with no more than one error but wrong answer given. Do not award any marks if the 0 for multiplying by a ten is missing. Do not award any marks if no final answer is given.)

32. $\frac{3}{20}$ (Accept equivalent fractions)

(1 mark)

33.

```
            2 2 5
  3 5 | 7 8 7 5
        7 0
        8 7 5
        7 0
        1 7 5
        1 7 5
              0
```

(2 marks for correct answer. Award 1 mark for using long division with no more than one error but wrong answer given. Do not award any marks if no final answer is given.)

34. $10\frac{3}{20}$ **(1 mark)**

35. $\frac{1}{15}$ **(1 mark)**

36. 50.993 **(1 mark)**

Set A Paper 2

1. 13, 25, 33, 45 and 53 circled only.
   (2 marks: 1 mark for three answers circled)

2. Any suitable answer, e.g.

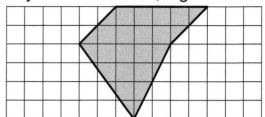

(2 marks: 1 mark for a shape with five sides; 1 mark for a pair of parallel lines)

3. $\frac{1}{2}$ (Accept $\frac{4}{8}$ or other equivalent fractions) **(1 mark)**

4. 11°C **(1 mark)**
   Athens and Berlin ticked only.
   (1 mark: 1 mark for both correct answers)

5.

```
  5 [0] 4 [6]
+ [7] 5 [5] 4
  1 2 6 0 0
```

(1 mark: all correct for 1 mark)

6. 64 cm **(1 mark)**

7. 8, 4 **(1 mark)**

8. 460,305 **(1 mark)**

9.

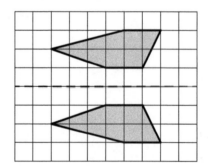

(Accept lines drawn to within 2 mm of vertices) **(1 mark)**

10. 15.4 pounds **(1 mark)**
   10 kg **(1 mark)**

11. 48,139 − (15,246 + 10,744 + 9,833) = 12,316

(2 marks for correct answer. Award 1 mark for correct working with wrong answer.)

12. 12 × 24 = 288; 288 × 8 = 2,304

(2 marks for correct answer. Award 1 mark for correct working, but wrong answer given.)

13. 5 : 3 = 60 : 36

60 ÷ 5 = 12

(2 marks for correct answer. Award 1 mark for correct working with wrong answer.)

14. 41.25 **(1 mark)**

15. 40

(3 marks for correct answer. Award 1 mark for finding 40% of 460 = 184 or 1 mark for finding 60% of 240 = 144 or 1 mark for a correct subtraction of the answers even if the percentages are incorrect.)

16. 11 **(1 mark)**

45 **(1 mark)**

17. □ = 12, △ = 6

(1 mark: 1 mark for both correct answers)

18. B **(1 mark)**

100 ml or 0.1 *l* **(1 mark)**

19. 210° **(1 mark)**

20. 24 and 48 **(1 mark)**

15 and 30 **(1 mark)**

7 and 53 **(1 mark)**

21. 13°C (Accept +/− 1°C) **(1 mark)**

September and October **(1 mark)**

Set A Paper 3

1. 740 or 650 or 641 **(1 mark)**

2. 4 **(1 mark)**

3. 7:20 (Accept 7:20 am, 7:20 pm, 07:20, 19:20, 20 past 7) **(1 mark)**

4.

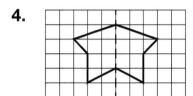

(Accept lines drawn to within 2 mm of vertices. Ignore lines that are not straight.) **(1 mark)**

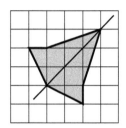

(Accept lines drawn within 2 mm of the vertices.) **(1 mark)**

5. 217 − 83 = 134;

134 + 350 = 484 minutes

(2 marks for correct answer. Award 1 mark for correct working, but wrong answer given.)

6. £5.20 (Do not accept 5.2) **(1 mark)**

7. 30 cm **(1 mark)**

Explanation should show that 1 yard is shorter than 1 metre; there are approximately 90 cm (3 × 30 cm) in 1 yard and 90 cm < 100 cm **(1 mark)**

8. 8°C **(1 mark)**

9. 2 and 29 (Accept answers in either order) **(1 mark)**

41   43   47 **(1 mark)**

10. $(\frac{1}{4} \times 24) + (\frac{1}{3} \times 24) + (\frac{3}{8} \times 24) = 23$;

$6 + 8 + 9 = 23$; $24 - 23 = 1$

(2 marks for correct answer. Award 1 mark for correct working, but wrong answer given.)

11. 600,000 **(1 mark)**

12. 5,634,721 **(1 mark)**

51,234 **(1 mark)**

13. 55° (Accept angles within 2°) **(1 mark)**

14. 275,386 – (54,895 + 143,706) = 76,785

(2 marks for correct answer. Award 1 mark for correct working, but wrong answer given.)

15. $\frac{3}{5} = \frac{12}{20}$ and $\frac{1}{4} = \frac{5}{20}$;

$1 - \frac{12}{20} - \frac{5}{20} = \frac{3}{20}$

(2 marks for correct answer. Award 1 mark for correct working, but wrong answer given.)

16. 2,550 g 2.5 kg 2.05 kg

2.005 kg 200 g (Accept units that have been converted correctly, e.g. 2,550 g 2,500 g 2,050 g 2005 g 200 g) **(1 mark)**

17. $x = 7.5$ cm **(1 mark)**

$y = 15$ cm **(1 mark)**

18. 350 × 30 = 10,500; 12 × 1,000 = 12,000; 12,000 – 10,500 = 1,500 ml

or 350 × 30 = 10,500; 10,500 ÷ 1000 = 10.5; 12 – 10.5 = 1.5 litres

(3 marks for a correct answer. 2 marks for sight of 10,500 or 10.5 or a correct method with only one arithmetic error. 1 mark for evidence of a correct method.)

19. 30 (Accept +/– 1) **(1 mark)**

120° **(1 mark)**

20 **(1 mark)**

20. 270 **(1 mark)**

21. 80 = 2*l* + 2 × 10; 80 = 2*l* + 20;

60 = 2*l*; 60 ÷ 2 = *l* = 30 cm

(2 marks for correct answer. Award 1 mark for correct working, but wrong answer given.)

Set B Paper 1

1. 8 **(1 mark)**

2. 4,745 **(1 mark)**

3. $\frac{3}{8}$ (Accept equivalent fractions) **(1 mark)**

4. 15 **(1 mark)**

5. 1,888 **(1 mark)**

6. 1,332 **(1 mark)**

7. 153 **(1 mark)**

8. 60 **(1 mark)**

9. 3,907 **(1 mark)**

10. 27 **(1 mark)**

11. 24,528 **(1 mark)**

12. 90,000 **(1 mark)**

13. 0.18 **(1 mark)**

14. $\frac{2}{5}$ (Accept $\frac{4}{10}$ and other equivalent fractions) **(1 mark)**

15. 5.4 **(1 mark)**

16. 330.47 **(1 mark)**

17. 72,000 **(1 mark)**

18. $\frac{1}{20}$ (Accept equivalent fractions) **(1 mark)**

19. 8,615 **(1 mark)**

20. 28.66 **(1 mark)**

21. $5\frac{3}{8}$ (Accept equivalent fractions. Accept $\frac{43}{8}$) **(1 mark)**

22. 24,000 **(1 mark)**

23. 900 **(1 mark)**

24. 0.075 **(1 mark)**

25. 613.43 **(1 mark)**

26.

```
          1  8  2
    ×        6  2
          3  6  4
    1  0  9  2  0
    1  1  2  8  4
```

(2 marks for correct answer. Award 1 mark for using long multiplication with no more than one error but wrong answer given. Do not award any marks if the 0 for multiplying by a ten is missing. Do not award any marks if no final answer is given.)

27. 250 (1 mark)

28.

```
             3  2
    2  2 | 7  0  4
          6  6
             4  4
             4  4
                0
```

(2 marks for correct answer. Award 1 mark for using long division with no more than one error but wrong answer given. Do not award any marks if no final answer is given.)

29. 60 (1 mark)

30.

```
                2  1
    7  1 | 1  4  9  1
          1  4  2
                7  1
                7  1
                   0
```

(2 marks for correct answer. Award 1 mark for using long division with no more than one error but wrong answer given. Do not award any marks if no final answer is given.)

31. $1\frac{1}{15}$ (Accept equivalent fractions) (1 mark)

32.

```
          3  0  7  4
    ×           3  5
    1  5  3  7  0
    9  2  2  2  0
    1  0  7  5  9  0
```

(2 marks for correct answer. Award 1 mark for using long multiplication with no more than one error but wrong answer given. Do not award any marks if the 0 for multiplying by a ten is missing. Do not award any marks if no final answer is given.)

33. 3,600,000 (1 mark)

34. 72.307 (1 mark)

35. 24 (1 mark)

36. $\frac{1}{3}$ (Accept equivalent fractions) (1 mark)

Set B Paper 2

1.

(1 mark: all three right angles needed for 1 mark)

2. 2 : 3 and 3 : 2 (Accept answers in either order)
(1 mark: 1 mark for both correct answers)

3. A bar or line drawn to show 8 (1 mark)

4. 16 or 2 × 8 (1 mark)

5. 112 packets (1 mark)

6. (10, 10) (1 mark)

7. 12 ÷ 3 = 4; 12 + 4 = 16 tins
(2 marks for correct answer. Award 1 mark for correct working, but wrong answer given.)

8. 20 ÷ 8 = 2.5; 600 × 2.5 = 1500 kg
(2 marks for correct answer. Award 1 mark for correct working, but wrong answer given.)

9. 500
10

(2 marks for correct answer. Award
1 mark for sight of: 56 + 64 = 120 or
3 × 4 = 12 or 120 ÷ 12) **(1 mark)**

10. Accept any correct answer, e.g.
456 ÷ 100 = 4.56; 465 ÷ 100 = 4.65;
546 ÷ 100 = 5.46; 564 ÷ 100 = 5.64;
645 ÷ 100 = 6.45; 654 ÷ 100 = 6.54
(1 mark)

11. 180° **(1 mark)**

12. £27.81

(3 marks for correct answer.
Award 1 mark for a correct method of
finding the cost of 9 adult and 3 child
tickets with a wrong answer and award
1 mark for a correct method of finding
the difference between the cost of the
individual tickets and the group ticket
with a wrong answer.)

13. 5   6   7   8   9

(2 marks: 2 marks for five correct
answers, 1 mark for three or four
correct answers)

14. −12   −21

(2 marks: 1 mark for each correct
answer)

15. 346,766 **(1 mark)**

16. 2°C **(1 mark)**
9°C **(1 mark)**

17. 30 + 5 = 35; 35 × 8 = 280; 0.75 × 80 =
60; 280 + 60 = £340

(2 marks: Award 1 mark for any
correct working with 280 or 60 seen,
but wrong answer given.)

18. Accept $\frac{1}{2} \times \frac{1}{8}$ or $\frac{1}{8} \times \frac{1}{2}$ or $\frac{1}{4} \times \frac{1}{4}$
or $\frac{1}{1} \times \frac{1}{16}$ or $\frac{1}{16} \times \frac{1}{1}$ **(1 mark)**

19. Dev takes £15
Sam takes £30 **(1 mark)**

20. Possible answers are:
length   24 cm   width   1 cm
length   12 cm   width   2 cm
length   6 cm   width   4 cm
(Accept lengths and widths reversed.
Accept fractions and decimals if
correct, e.g. 48 cm × 0.5 cm. Do not
accept length 3 cm, width 8 cm)
(2 marks: 1 mark for each pair of
correct answers)

21. 135° **(1 mark)**

22. rectangle (Accept oblong) **(1 mark)**
parallelogram **(1 mark)**

23. 1,920 cm³ **(1 mark)**

Set B Paper 3

1. Possible answers: 567 + 34,
564 + 37, 537 + 64, 534 + 67
(2 marks: 1 mark for correct placing of
7 and 4 in the units column)

2. 2nd and 3rd boxes ticked only.
(2 marks: 1 mark for each correct
box ticked)

3. 29 games **(1 mark)**
10 games **(1 mark)**

4. 3rd and 5th boxes ticked only.
(2 marks: 1 mark for each correct
box ticked; 1 mark if two correct
and one incorrect box ticked)

5. 10 − (2.3 + 1.6) = 6.1 kg or 10,000 −
(2,300 + 1,600) = 6,100 g (Accept 6.1 kg
or 6100 g. Units must be correct, e.g.
do not accept 6.1 g or 6,100 kg. Accept
6,100 or 6.1 without units.)
(2 marks for correct answer. Award
1 mark for correct working, but wrong
answer given.)

6.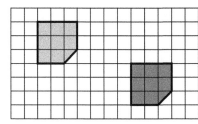

(2 marks: 2 marks for drawing as shown; 1 mark for correctly orientated and sized shape translated 7 units right or 3 units down)

7. 2 years (Accept II years) **(1 mark)**

8. 36 circled only. **(1 mark)**

9. $3.5 \times 1{,}000 = 3{,}500$; $3{,}500 \div 50 = 70\,m^2$

(2 marks for correct answer. Award 1 mark for correct working, but wrong answer given.)

10. $1 - \frac{4}{5} = \frac{1}{5}$ are red; $800 \div 5 = 160$ counters

(2 marks for correct answer. Award 1 mark for correct working, but wrong answer given.)

11. 53

42

31

(2 marks: 2 marks for three correct answers, 1 mark for one correct answer)

12. 2nd box ticked only. **(1 mark)**

13. $2{,}500 \times 3 = 7{,}500$ points available on other three levels; $7{,}500 + 5{,}450 = 12{,}950$ points

(2 marks for correct answer. Award 1 mark for correct working, but wrong answer given.)

14. 63°C **(1 mark)**

15. Paper 1   70% **(1 mark)**

Paper 2   72% **(1 mark)**

16. $\dfrac{80 - (\frac{1}{4} \times 80 + 30)}{2} = 15$ children

(2 marks for correct answer. Award 1 mark for correct working, but wrong answer given.)

17. 1 large square + 2 small squares = 45; 2 large squares + 2 small squares = 80; so 1 large square = 80 − 45 = 35; 2 small squares therefore = 10 (5 each); new pattern therefore = 35 + 35 + 10 + 10 = 90

(2 marks for correct answer. Award 1 mark for evidence of a correct method with 35, 70, 10 or 5 seen.)

18. 150 cm² **(1 mark)**

19. D   (−4, 1) **(1 mark)**

E   (−8, −1) **(1 mark)**

20. $110 \div 8 = 13.75$;

$17.5(0) - 13.75 = £3.75$

(2 marks for correct answer. Award 1 mark for correct working, but wrong answer given.)

THIS PAGE HAS INTENTIONALLY BEEN LEFT BLANK